Table of Contents

1. Introduction

    o   Overview of the Project
    o   Prerequisites

2. Setting Up the Development Environment

    o   Installing Python
    o   Installing PyCharm
    o   Installing Required Libraries

3. Designing the Database

    o   Overview of Database Design
    o   Setting Up SQLite
    o   Creating the Comic Book Database Schema

4. Creating the GUI with Tkinter

    o   Introduction to Tkinter
    o   Designing the Main Window
    o   Adding GUI Elements (Labels, Entry Fields, Buttons)

1. Implementing CRUD Operations

    o   Adding a Comic Book Entry
    o   Viewing and Searching Comic Books
    o   Editing a Comic Book Entry

- Deleting a Comic Book Entry

2. Adding Additional Features

    - Implementing a Web-Crawler to Check Current Market Values
    - Adding an Image Upload Feature

3. Testing and Debugging

    - Unit Testing
    - Debugging Tips

4. Finalizing the Application

    - Packaging the Application
    - Deployment Options

5. Conclusion and Next Steps

Chapter 1: Introduction to Programming a Comic Book Database

The world of comic books is rich with history, art, and storytelling, making it an ideal domain for exploring database management and programming. Whether you're a comic book collector, a programmer looking for a practical project, or someone curious about how databases work, this project is an excellent way to combine technology with creativity.

In this chapter, we'll discuss the goals of the project, provide an overview of what you'll create, and outline the features of the comic book database application.

1.1 Project Goals

This project will guide you through the development of a fully functional comic book database system using Python and PyCharm. By the end, you'll have created an application that allows users to:

1. Store Comic Book Information:

    Title, publisher, issue number, series, face price, and quantity.

2. Check Current Market Values:

    Use a web-crawler to retrieve current comic book values online.

3. Manage Comic Entries:

    Add, edit, search, and delete entries in the database.

4. Upload Cover Images:

Include visual representations of comic book covers for each entry.

5. Create a User-Friendly GUI:

   Design an intuitive interface that simplifies database interactions.

This project provides a hands-on way to learn Python programming concepts, database management, GUI development, and web scraping.

1.2 Why Use Python and PyCharm?

Python is an ideal choice for this project due to its simplicity, versatility, and extensive library support. Here's why Python and PyCharm are the perfect combination for this task:

1. Python:
   - Easy-to-learn syntax makes it accessible for beginners.
   - Extensive libraries like sqlite3, tkinter, and requests streamline development.
   - Cross-platform compatibility ensures your application can run on Windows, macOS, and Linux.

2. PyCharm:
   - A powerful IDE with features like code completion, debugging tools, and version control.
   - Simplifies managing dependencies and organizing your project.
   - Enhances productivity with an integrated terminal, database tools, and visualization features.

1.3 Overview of the Application

The comic book database system combines several programming concepts and technologies. Here's a breakdown of the core components:

1. Database Management:

   The system uses SQLite, a lightweight and easy-to-use database, to store comic book information. You'll learn how to design a database schema, interact with the database, and implement CRUD (Create, Read, Update, Delete) operations.

2. Graphical User Interface (GUI):

   The user interface is built with Tkinter, Python's standard GUI toolkit. You'll create a visually appealing and user-friendly interface that allows users to manage their comic collection effortlessly.

3. Web Crawling:

   A web crawler, implemented using the requests and BeautifulSoup libraries, will fetch real-time market values for comic books from online sources.

4. Image Management:

   Using the Pillow library, the application will allow users to upload and display cover images for their comics.

1.4 Features of the Comic Book Database

The application will include the following features:

1. Adding Comic Books:

   Users can input details such as title, publisher, issue number, series, face price, and quantity.

2. Viewing and Searching Entries:

   A table view displays all stored comics, with options to filter results by title, publisher, or series.

3. Editing Entries:

   Users can update the details of any comic book in their collection.

4. Deleting Entries:

   Entries can be removed individually or in bulk, giving users complete control over their database.

5. Checking Current Values:

   The web crawler retrieves up-to-date market values for comics, keeping users informed about their collection's worth.

6. Uploading Cover Images:

   Users can upload an image of the comic book cover, which will be displayed alongside its details.

1. Intuitive GUI:

1.3 Overview of the Application

The comic book database system combines several programming concepts and technologies. Here's a breakdown of the core components:

1. Database Management:

   The system uses SQLite, a lightweight and easy-to-use database, to store comic book information. You'll learn how to design a database schema, interact with the database, and implement CRUD (Create, Read, Update, Delete) operations.

2. Graphical User Interface (GUI):

   The user interface is built with Tkinter, Python's standard GUI toolkit. You'll create a visually appealing and user-friendly interface that allows users to manage their comic collection effortlessly.

3. Web Crawling:

   A web crawler, implemented using the requests and BeautifulSoup libraries, will fetch real-time market values for comic books from online sources.

4. Image Management:

   Using the Pillow library, the application will allow users to upload and display cover images for their comics.

1.4 Features of the Comic Book Database

The application will include the following features:

1. Adding Comic Books:

   Users can input details such as title, publisher, issue number, series, face price, and quantity.

2. Viewing and Searching Entries:

   A table view displays all stored comics, with options to filter results by title, publisher, or series.

3. Editing Entries:

   Users can update the details of any comic book in their collection.

4. Deleting Entries:

   Entries can be removed individually or in bulk, giving users complete control over their database.

5. Checking Current Values:

   The web crawler retrieves up-to-date market values for comics, keeping users informed about their collection's worth.

6. Uploading Cover Images:

   Users can upload an image of the comic book cover, which will be displayed alongside its details.

1. Intuitive GUI:

The application will feature a clean and modern interface, making it accessible even for non-technical users.

1.5 Skills You'll Learn

This project is designed to teach practical programming and database management skills. By the end of this e-book, you'll have gained experience in:

1. Python Programming:

   Master core Python concepts, including functions, classes, and file handling.

2. Database Design and Management:

   Learn how to design a relational database schema and interact with SQLite databases using Python.

3. GUI Development:

   Build a graphical interface with Tkinter, learning to create layouts, handle user input, and display data dynamically.

4. Web Scraping:

   Use libraries like requests and BeautifulSoup to extract and parse data from web pages.

5. Image Handling:

   Implement image upload and display functionality using the Pillow library.

6. Project Development Workflow:

   Follow best practices for organizing code, managing dependencies, and debugging.

1.6 The Importance of Data Management

Databases are the backbone of modern applications, enabling efficient data storage, retrieval, and manipulation. Whether you're managing a comic book collection, an e-commerce platform, or a customer database, understanding how databases work is a critical skill for any developer.

By working on this project, you'll not only learn how to build a database system but also develop a deeper appreciation for the role of data in everyday applications.

1.7 What's Next?

In the next chapter, we'll set up the development environment, install the required tools, and create a blueprint for the comic book database system. By the end of Chapter 2, you'll be ready to start building the foundation of your application.

Chapter 2: Setting Up the Development Environment

Before diving into the programming of the comic book database application, it's essential to set up the tools and libraries needed for development. This chapter will guide you through installing Python, setting up PyCharm, and configuring the necessary libraries. By the end of this chapter, you'll have a fully functional environment ready to start building your application.

2.1 Installing Python

Python is the primary programming language we'll use for this project. Follow these steps to install Python:

1. Download Python:

    - Visit the official Python website.
    - Download the latest version compatible with your operating system (Windows, macOS, or Linux).

2. Install Python:

    - Run the downloaded installer.
    - On the installation screen, ensure you check the box labeled Add Python to PATH (important for command-line use).
    - Click Install Now and follow the prompts.

3. Verify Installation:

    - Open a terminal or command prompt and type:

    bash

    Copy code

python --version

- This should display the installed Python version.

2.2 Installing PyCharm

PyCharm is a powerful Integrated Development Environment (IDE) designed for Python programming. Follow these steps to set up PyCharm:

1. Download PyCharm:

    - Visit the PyCharm download page.
    - Download the Community Edition (free and sufficient for this project).

2. Install PyCharm:

    - Run the installer and follow the setup wizard.
    - During installation, choose to create a desktop shortcut for easy access.
    - Launch PyCharm once installation is complete.

3. Initial Configuration:

    - On the welcome screen, select New Project.
    - Choose a directory for your project and set the Python interpreter (PyCharm will detect the Python installation automatically).
    - Click Create to set up the project.

2.3 Installing Required Python Libraries

To build the comic book database application, we'll use several Python libraries. These libraries provide the tools needed for database management, GUI creation, web scraping, and image handling.

Step 1: Open the Terminal in PyCharm

In PyCharm, go to View > Tool Windows > Terminal to open the terminal within the IDE.

Step 2: Install Libraries

Run the following commands in the terminal to install the required libraries:

1. Tkinter: For creating the graphical user interface.

   Tkinter comes pre-installed with Python, so no additional installation is needed.

2. SQLite: For database management.

   SQLite is built into Python's standard library and requires no installation.

3. Requests and BeautifulSoup: For web scraping.

   bash

   Copy code

   pip install requests pip install beautifulsoup4

4. Pillow: For image handling.

   bash

   Copy code

   pip install pillow

1. PyInstaller: For packaging the application into an executable file.

```bash
Copy code

pip install pyinstaller
```

2. **Additional Tools:** If additional libraries are needed during development, you can install them using the same method.

2.4 Setting Up the Project Structure

Organizing your project files is essential for maintainability. Below is the suggested structure for the comic book database application:

```plaintext
Copy code

comic_book_database/
├── main.py           # Main application file
├── database/
│   ├── init.py       # Makes this a package
│   ├── db_setup.py   # Database schema and setup
│   └── db_operations.py  # CRUD operations
├── gui/
│   ├── init.py       # Makes this a package
│   └── gui_design.py # Tkinter GUI design
├── web_scraper/
│   ├── init.py       # Makes this a package
│   └── scraper.py    # Web scraping logic
├── images/           # Folder for comic book cover images
├── tests/            # Unit tests for the application
│   ├── init.py
│   └── test_db.py    # Tests for database operations
└── README.md         # Project documentation
```

2.5 Configuring PyCharm for Development

1. **Set Up Virtual Environment (Optional but Recommended):**
   - PyCharm can create a virtual environment for your project, isolating its dependencies.

- Go to File > Settings > Project > Python Interpreter, click the gear icon, and select Add... > New Virtualenv Environment.
- Choose the base interpreter (Python installation) and click OK.

2. Enable Version Control:

    - If you plan to use Git for version control, initialize a Git repository in your project.
    - Go to VCS > Enable Version Control Integration, and select Git.
    - Use GitHub or another repository hosting service to back up your code.

3. Install Additional Plugins (Optional):

You can install helpful plugins, such as Database Navigator for database management and Markdown Support for editing your README file.

2.6 Testing the Setup

Create a simple "Hello, World!" program to ensure everything is working correctly.

1. Write the Code:

    Open main.py and add the following:

    python

    Copy code

    import tkinter as tk # Create the main window root = tk.Tk() root.title("Comic Book Database")

```
root.geometry("400x300") # Add a label label = tk.Label(root, text="Hello, Comic Book World!", font=("Arial", 16)) label.pack(pady=50) # Run the application root.mainloop()
```

2. Run the Program:

    - Click the green Run button in PyCharm.
    - A window should appear displaying the message, "Hello, Comic Book World!"

2.7 Common Issues and Troubleshooting

1. Python Not Found:

    Ensure Python is added to the system PATH during installation. Reinstall Python if necessary.

2. Library Installation Errors:

    - Check the terminal output for specific error messages.
    - Ensure you're connected to the internet and have the correct pip version by running:

    bash

    Copy code

    python -m ensurepip --upgrade

3. Tkinter Errors:

If Tkinter is not recognized, verify that your Python installation includes it. Some Linux distributions require installing Tkinter separately:

```bash
```

Copy code

```
sudo apt-get install python3-tk
```

2.8 What's Next?

With the development environment set up, you're ready to start building the foundation of your comic book database application. In the next chapter, we'll design the database schema and implement the initial setup using SQLite.

Chapter 3: Designing the Database

A well-designed database is the backbone of any data-driven application. In this chapter, we'll create the database schema for the comic book database application using SQLite. You'll learn how to set up the database, define the structure, and prepare it for integration with the Python program.

3.1 What is a Database?

A database is a structured collection of data that allows for efficient storage, retrieval, and management. In this project, we'll use SQLite, a lightweight, serverless database engine ideal for small to medium-sized applications.

3.2 Choosing SQLite for the Comic Book Database

SQLite is an excellent choice for this project because:

1. Lightweight and Easy to Use: No server installation or configuration is required.
2. Built into Python: Python's standard library includes SQLite, making it easy to integrate.
3. Self-Contained: The entire database is stored in a single .db file, simplifying deployment.

3.3 Planning the Database Schema

The database schema defines the structure of the database, including the tables and their fields. For the comic book database, we'll create a single table named comic_books with the following columns:

Column NameData TypeDescriptionidINTEGERPrimary key (auto-incremented).titleTEXTTitle of the comic book.publisherTEXTPublisher of the comic book.issueTEXTIssue number.seriesTEXTName of the comic book series.face_priceREALOriginal price of the comic.quantityINTEGERNumber of copies owned.current_valueREALCurrent market value (retrieved via web).cover_imageTEXTFile path for the cover image.

3.4 Setting Up the Database

Step 1: Import the Required Module

Python's sqlite3 library is used to interact with SQLite databases. Import it at the beginning of your script.

python

Copy code

```
import sqlite3
```

Step 2: Create the Database File

Use the following script to create a new SQLite database file named comics.db:

python

Copy code

Create a connection to the SQLite database # If the database does not exist, it will be created conn = sqlite3.connect('comics.db') # Create a cursor object to interact with the database cursor = conn.cursor()

Step 3: Define the Schema

Write the SQL command to create the comic_books table:

python

Copy code

```python
# SQL command to create the comic_books table
create_table_query = '''
CREATE TABLE IF NOT EXISTS comic_books (
    id INTEGER PRIMARY KEY AUTOINCREMENT,
    title TEXT NOT NULL,
    publisher TEXT NOT NULL,
    issue TEXT NOT NULL,
    series TEXT NOT NULL,
    face_price REAL NOT NULL,
    quantity INTEGER NOT NULL,
    current_value REAL,
    cover_image TEXT
)
'''
# Execute the SQL command
cursor.execute(create_table_query)
# Commit changes and close the connection
conn.commit()
conn.close()
print("Database and table created successfully!")
```

3.5 Testing the Database Setup

1. Run the Script:

    - Save the script as db_setup.py and run it using PyCharm or the command line:

        bash

        Copy code

        ```bash
        python db_setup.py
        ```

    - This will create the comics.db file and the comic_books table.

2. Verify the Database:

Open the database file using an SQLite viewer (e.g., DB Browser for SQLite) to confirm that the comic_books table has been created.

3.6 Inserting Sample Data

Let's add some sample data to the database for testing purposes:

python

Copy code

```
# Connect to the database conn = sqlite3.connect('comics.db') cursor = conn.cursor() # Insert sample data sample_data = [ ("Batman #1", "DC Comics", "1", "Batman", 0.10, 1, None, None), ("Amazing Fantasy #15", "Marvel Comics", "15", "Amazing Fantasy", 0.12, 1, None, None), ("Superman #1", "DC Comics", "1", "Superman", 0.10, 2, None, None) ] # SQL command to insert data insert_query = ''' INSERT INTO comic_books (title, publisher, issue, series, face_price, quantity, current_value, cover_image) VALUES (?, ?, ?, ?, ?, ?, ?, ?) ''' # Execute the command for each row for comic in sample_data: cursor.execute(insert_query, comic) # Commit changes and close the connection conn.commit() conn.close() print("Sample data inserted successfully!")
```

3.7 Retrieving Data from the Database

To retrieve and display data from the database, use the following script:

python

Copy code

```
# Connect to the database conn = sqlite3.connect('comics.db') cursor = conn.cursor() # SQL command to select all data select_query = '''
```

SELECT * FROM comic_books ''' # Execute the command and fetch all rows cursor.execute(select_query) rows = cursor.fetchall() # Display the data for row in rows: print(row) # Close the connection conn.close()

3.8 Structuring Database Operations in a Separate Module

To keep the project organized, we'll create a db_operations.py file to handle database interactions. This module will include functions for adding, retrieving, updating, and deleting data.

Example:

python

Copy code

def add_comic(title, publisher, issue, series, face_price, quantity, current_value, cover_image): conn = sqlite3.connect('comics.db') cursor = conn.cursor() cursor.execute(''' INSERT INTO comic_books (title, publisher, issue, series, face_price, quantity, current_value, cover_image) VALUES (?, ?, ?, ?, ?, ?, ?, ?) ''', (title, publisher, issue, series, face_price, quantity, current_value, cover_image)) conn.commit() conn.close() print("Comic added successfully!")

3.9 Database Best Practices

1. Use Parameterized Queries:

   Avoid SQL injection by using parameterized queries (? placeholders) instead of directly concatenating strings.

2. Close Connections:

Always close the database connection after operations to prevent memory leaks.

3. Error Handling:

   Wrap database operations in try-except blocks to handle errors gracefully.

3.10 What's Next?

Now that the database is set up and functional, the next step is to design the graphical user interface (GUI) for the application. In the next chapter, you'll learn how to create a user-friendly GUI using Tkinter and integrate it with the database.

Chapter 4: Creating the GUI with Tkinter

A graphical user interface (GUI) is essential for creating a user-friendly application. In this chapter, we'll use Tkinter, Python's standard GUI toolkit, to design and implement the interface for the comic book database system. By the end of this chapter, you'll have a functional interface where users can input data, view records, and interact with the database.

4.1 Introduction to Tkinter

Tkinter is a built-in Python library that provides tools to create GUI applications. Here's why we're using Tkinter for this project:

- Ease of Use: Tkinter is straightforward and beginner-friendly.
- Cross-Platform Compatibility: Applications created with Tkinter run on Windows, macOS, and Linux.
- Extensibility: Tkinter supports a wide range of widgets, including buttons, labels, text fields, and tables.

4.2 Setting Up the Main Application Window

The main application window is the foundation of your GUI. Let's create it with basic configuration:

python

Copy code

import tkinter as tk from tkinter import ttk # Create the main application window root = tk.Tk() root.title("Comic Book Database") root.geometry("800x600") # Set the window size # Add a title label title_label = tk.Label(root, text="Comic Book Database", font=("Arial", 24)) title_label.pack(pady=10) # Add padding around the label # Run the Tkinter main loop root.mainloop()

4.3 Adding Input Fields for Comic Data

Input fields allow users to enter comic book details. Use Label and Entry widgets to create these fields.

python

Copy code

```
# Frame for input fields input_frame = tk.Frame(root)
input_frame.pack(pady=20) # Title title_label = tk.Label(input_frame, text="Title:") title_label.grid(row=0, column=0, padx=5, pady=5, sticky="e") title_entry = tk.Entry(input_frame, width=30) title_entry.grid(row=0, column=1, padx=5, pady=5) # Publisher publisher_label = tk.Label(input_frame, text="Publisher:") publisher_label.grid(row=1, column=0, padx=5, pady=5, sticky="e") publisher_entry = tk.Entry(input_frame, width=30) publisher_entry.grid(row=1, column=1, padx=5, pady=5) # Issue Number issue_label = tk.Label(input_frame, text="Issue Number:") issue_label.grid(row=2, column=0, padx=5, pady=5, sticky="e") issue_entry = tk.Entry(input_frame, width=30) issue_entry.grid(row=2, column=1, padx=5, pady=5) # Repeat for other fields (series, face price, quantity, etc.)
```

4.4 Adding Buttons for User Actions

Buttons allow users to trigger specific actions, such as adding a new comic or searching for records.

python

Copy code

```
# Frame for action buttons button_frame = tk.Frame(root)
button_frame.pack(pady=20) # Add Comic Button add_button = tk.Button(button_frame, text="Add Comic", command=lambda:
```

add_comic()) add_button.grid(row=0, column=0, padx=10) # View Comics Button view_button = tk.Button(button_frame, text="View Comics", command=lambda: view_comics()) view_button.grid(row=0, column=1, padx=10) # Delete Comic Button delete_button = tk.Button(button_frame, text="Delete Comic", command=lambda: delete_comic()) delete_button.grid(row=0, column=2, padx=10)

4.5 Displaying Data in a Table

We'll use the ttk.Treeview widget to display comic book records in a table format.

python

Copy code

Frame for table view table_frame = tk.Frame(root) table_frame.pack(pady=20) # Treeview Widget columns = ("ID", "Title", "Publisher", "Issue", "Series", "Face Price", "Quantity", "Current Value", "Cover Image") tree = ttk.Treeview(table_frame, columns=columns, show="headings", height=10) # Define column headings for col in columns: tree.heading(col, text=col) tree.column(col, width=100, anchor="center") tree.pack()

4.6 Integrating Database Operations

Now let's connect the GUI with the database. For example, adding a new comic:

1. Define the add_comic Function:

   python

   Copy code

```python
import sqlite3
def add_comic():
    title = title_entry.get()
    publisher = publisher_entry.get()
    issue = issue_entry.get()
    # Get other fields...
    conn = sqlite3.connect('comics.db')
    cursor = conn.cursor()
    cursor.execute("' INSERT INTO comic_books (title, publisher, issue, series, face_price, quantity) VALUES (?, ?, ?, ?, ?, ?) '", (title, publisher, issue, series_entry.get(), float(face_price_entry.get()), int(quantity_entry.get())))
    conn.commit()
    conn.close()
    print("Comic added successfully!")
    clear_entries()
```

2. Clear Input Fields After Submission:

python

Copy code

```python
def clear_entries():
    title_entry.delete(0, tk.END)
    publisher_entry.delete(0, tk.END)
    issue_entry.delete(0, tk.END)
    # Repeat for other fields...
```

4.7 Adding Navigation Features

Enhance user experience by allowing easy navigation between sections:

- Search Functionality:

python

Copy code

```python
def search_comics():
    search_term = search_entry.get()
    conn = sqlite3.connect('comics.db')
    cursor = conn.cursor()
    cursor.execute("SELECT * FROM comic_books WHERE title LIKE ?", ('%' + search_term + '%',))
    rows = cursor.fetchall()
    update_table(rows)
    conn.close()
```

- Update Table:

python

Copy code

def update_table(data): for row in tree.get_children(): tree.delete(row) for record in data: tree.insert('', tk.END, values=record)

4.8 Adding Cover Image Upload

Add a feature to upload cover images using the filedialog module:

python

Copy code

from tkinter import filedialog from PIL import Image, ImageTk def upload_image(): file_path = filedialog.askopenfilename(filetypes=[("Image files", "*.jpg *.png")]) cover_image_entry.insert(0, file_path) img = Image.open(file_path) img.thumbnail((100, 100)) img_tk = ImageTk.PhotoImage(img) img_label = tk.Label(root, image=img_tk) img_label.image = img_tk img_label.pack()

4.9 Refining the GUI Layout

1. Use Frames for Organization:

   Group related widgets into frames to make the layout cleaner.

2. Add Scrollbars:

If the table or text fields overflow, use scrollbars for better usability:

```python
```

Copy code

```python
scrollbar = ttk.Scrollbar(table_frame, orient="vertical", command=tree.yview) tree.configure(yscroll=scrollbar.set) scrollbar.pack(side="right", fill="y")
```

3. Improve Aesthetics:

   Add padding, colors, or fonts to enhance the appearance of the application:

```python
```

Copy code

```python
title_label.config(fg="blue", bg="lightgray", font=("Helvetica", 16, "bold"))
```

4.10 Testing the GUI

1. Run the GUI application:

   - Open PyCharm and run the main.py file.
   - Ensure all buttons and input fields respond correctly.

2. Verify database operations:

   Test adding, viewing, and deleting records using the GUI.

4.11 What's Next?

In the next chapter, we'll implement CRUD (Create, Read, Update, Delete) operations for managing comic book records and explore integrating advanced features like web crawling for current market values.

Chapter 5: Implementing CRUD Operations

CRUD operations—Create, Read, Update, and Delete—are the foundation of any database application. In this chapter, we'll implement these functions step by step, integrating them with the Tkinter GUI and the SQLite database. By the end of this chapter, users will be able to manage their comic book records efficiently.

5.1 What Are CRUD Operations?

CRUD operations allow users to perform basic data management tasks:

1. Create: Add new records to the database.
2. Read: Retrieve and display data from the database.
3. Update: Modify existing records.
4. Delete: Remove records from the database.

5.2 Adding Records (Create Operation)

Users can add new comic book entries via input fields in the GUI. This process involves capturing user input and inserting it into the database.

Step 1: Define the add_comic Function

Create a function to handle the addition of a new record.

python

Copy code

```python
import sqlite3
def add_comic():
    # Collect user input
    title = title_entry.get()
    publisher = publisher_entry.get()
    issue = issue_entry.get()
    series = series_entry.get()
    face_price = float(face_price_entry.get())
    quantity = int(quantity_entry.get())
    # Insert into the database
    conn = sqlite3.connect('comics.db')
    cursor = conn.cursor()
    cursor.execute("' INSERT INTO comic_books (title, publisher, issue, series, face_price, quantity) VALUES (?, ?, ?, ?, ?, ?) '", (title, publisher, issue, series, face_price, quantity))
    conn.commit()
    conn.close()
    # Clear input fields and update table
    clear_entries()
    view_comics()
    print("Comic added successfully!")
```

Step 2: Clear Input Fields

Define a helper function to clear the input fields after a comic is added.

python

Copy code

```
def clear_entries(): title_entry.delete(0, tk.END)
publisher_entry.delete(0, tk.END) issue_entry.delete(0, tk.END)
series_entry.delete(0, tk.END) face_price_entry.delete(0, tk.END)
quantity_entry.delete(0, tk.END)
```

Step 3: Connect the Button

Link the add_comic function to the Add Comic button in the GUI:

python

Copy code

add_button.config(command=add_comic)

5.3 Viewing Records (Read Operation)

The ttk.Treeview widget will display all comic book records in a table format.

Step 1: Define the view_comics Function

Fetch data from the database and display it in the table.

python

Copy code

```
def view_comics():
    # Connect to the database
    conn = sqlite3.connect('comics.db')
    cursor = conn.cursor()
    cursor.execute('SELECT FROM comic_books')
    rows = cursor.fetchall()
    conn.close()
    # Clear the table
    tree.delete(tree.get_children())
    # Insert new data into the table
    for row in rows:
        tree.insert('', tk.END, values=row)
```

Step 2: Connect the Button

Link the view_comics function to the View Comics button:

python

Copy code

view_button.config(command=view_comics)

5.4 Editing Records (Update Operation)

Users can select a record from the table, edit its details, and save the changes.

Step 1: Populate Fields for Editing

Define a function to populate input fields with the selected record's data.

python

Copy code

```
def select_comic(event):
    # Get selected record
    selected_item = tree.selection()[0]
    record = tree.item(selected_item, 'values')
    # Populate input fields
    title_entry.delete(0, tk.END)
    title_entry.insert(0, record[1])
    publisher_entry.delete(0, tk.END)
    publisher_entry.insert(0, record[2])
    issue_entry.delete(0, tk.END)
    issue_entry.insert(0, record[3])
    series_entry.delete(0, tk.END)
    series_entry.insert(0, record[4])
    face_price_entry.delete(0, tk.END)
    face_price_entry.insert(0, record[5])
    quantity_entry.delete(0, tk.END)
    quantity_entry.insert(0, record[6])
```

Bind the function to the table:

python

Copy code

```
tree.bind('<ButtonRelease-1>', select_comic)
```

Step 2: Define the update_comic Function

Update the selected record in the database.

python

Copy code

```python
def update_comic():
    selected_item = tree.selection()[0]
    record_id = tree.item(selected_item, 'values')[0]
    # Collect updated values
    title = title_entry.get()
    publisher = publisher_entry.get()
    issue = issue_entry.get()
    series = series_entry.get()
    face_price = float(face_price_entry.get())
    quantity = int(quantity_entry.get())
    # Update the database
    conn = sqlite3.connect('comics.db')
    cursor = conn.cursor()
    cursor.execute('''  UPDATE comic_books SET title = ?, publisher = ?, issue = ?, series = ?, face_price = ?, quantity = ? WHERE id = ? ''', (title, publisher, issue, series, face_price, quantity, record_id))
    conn.commit()
    conn.close()
    # Refresh the table
    view_comics()
    print("Comic updated successfully!")
```

Connect the Update button to the update_comic function:

python

Copy code

```python
update_button.config(command=update_comic)
```

5.5 Deleting Records (Delete Operation)

Users can delete selected records from the database.

Step 1: Define the delete_comic Function

Remove the selected record from the database.

python

Copy code

```python
def delete_comic(): selected_item = tree.selection()[0] record_id = tree.item(selected_item, 'values')[0] # Delete from the database conn = sqlite3.connect('comics.db') cursor = conn.cursor() cursor.execute('DELETE FROM comic_books WHERE id = ?', (record_id,)) conn.commit() conn.close() # Refresh the table view_comics() print("Comic deleted successfully!")
```

Step 2: Connect the Button

Link the Delete button to the delete_comic function:

python

Copy code

delete_button.config(command=delete_comic)

5.6 Testing CRUD Operations

1. Test Adding Records:

    - Enter data in the input fields and click Add Comic.
    - Verify that the record appears in the table.

2. Test Viewing Records:

    Click View Comics to ensure all records are displayed.

3. Test Editing Records:

    - Select a record, modify its details, and click Update.
    - Verify that the changes are reflected in the table.

4. Test Deleting Records:

    - Select a record and click Delete.
    - Verify that the record is removed.

5.7 Enhancing CRUD Operations

1. Search Functionality: Add a search bar to filter records by title or publisher.

2. Bulk Delete: Allow users to select and delete multiple records simultaneously.
3. Validation: Implement input validation to prevent errors (e.g., ensure numerical fields contain valid numbers).
4. Confirmation Prompts: Display confirmation dialogs before deleting records:

```python
```

Copy code

```
from tkinter import messagebox if messagebox.askyesno("Confirm Delete", "Are you sure you want to delete this record?"): delete_comic()
```

5.8 What's Next?

With CRUD operations implemented, the foundation of the application is complete. In the next chapter, we'll enhance the functionality by integrating a web crawler to fetch current market values for comic books.

Chapter 6: Adding Additional Features

In this chapter, we will implement advanced features to enhance the functionality and user experience of the comic book database application. Specifically, we will:

1. Add a web-crawler to fetch current market values for comic books.
2. Enable users to upload and display comic book cover images.
3. Integrate these features seamlessly into the GUI.

6.1 Implementing a Web-Crawler for Current Market Values

A web crawler retrieves data from a website. For this project, the crawler will fetch the current market value of a comic book based on its title. We'll use the requests and BeautifulSoup libraries for this task.

Step 1: Install Required Libraries

Ensure the libraries are installed:

bash

Copy code

pip install requests beautifulsoup4

Step 2: Define the Web-Crawler Function

The function will fetch data from a hypothetical comic book market website.

python

Copy code

```python
import requests
from bs4 import BeautifulSoup

def fetch_market_value(title):
    # Prepare the search URL
    search_query = title.replace(" ", "+")
    url = f"https://example-comic-pricing.com/search?q={search_query}"
    # Fetch the page content
    response = requests.get(url)
    if response.status_code != 200:
        print("Error: Unable to fetch market value")
        return None
    # Parse the HTML
    soup = BeautifulSoup(response.text, 'html.parser')
    # Extract the market value (adjust selector to match the actual site)
    try:
        value = soup.find("span", class_="current-price").text
        return float(value.replace("$", ""))
    except AttributeError:
        print("Error: Market value not found")
        return None
```

Step 3: Integrate with the GUI

Add a button to fetch the market value for the entered title:

python

Copy code

```python
def get_current_value():
    title = title_entry.get()
    if not title:
        print("Error: Title is required")
        return
    market_value = fetch_market_value(title)
    if market_value is not None:
        print(f"Current market value: ${market_value}")
        current_value_entry.delete(0, tk.END)
        current_value_entry.insert(0, market_value)
```

Add a button in the GUI:

python

Copy code

```python
fetch_button = tk.Button(button_frame, text="Fetch Market Value", command=get_current_value)
fetch_button.grid(row=0, column=3, padx=10)
```

6.2 Adding an Image Upload Feature

Users can upload images of comic book covers, which will be stored in the database and displayed in the GUI.

Step 1: Install the Pillow Library

Pillow is a Python imaging library for handling images:

```bash
```

Copy code

```
pip install pillow
```

Step 2: Define the Image Upload Function

This function will allow users to select an image file and store its path in the database.

python

Copy code

```python
from tkinter import filedialog
from PIL import Image, ImageTk
def upload_cover():
    file_path = filedialog.askopenfilename(filetypes=[("Image files", "*.jpg;*.png")])
    if file_path:
        cover_image_entry.delete(0, tk.END)
        cover_image_entry.insert(0, file_path)
        # Display the image in the GUI
        img = Image.open(file_path)
        img.thumbnail((100, 100))
        img_tk = ImageTk.PhotoImage(img)
        img_label = tk.Label(root, image=img_tk)
        img_label.image = img_tk  # Keep a reference to avoid garbage collection
        img_label.pack()
```

Step 3: Add the Image Path to the Database

Modify the add_comic function to include the image path:

python

Copy code

cover_image = cover_image_entry.get() cursor.execute("' INSERT INTO comic_books (title, publisher, issue, series, face_price, quantity, cover_image) VALUES (?, ?, ?, ?, ?, ?, ?) "', (title, publisher, issue, series, face_price, quantity, cover_image))

Step 4: Display Images in the GUI

Update the view_comics function to show the cover image for selected records.

python

Copy code

```python
def show_cover_image():
    selected_item = tree.selection()[0]
    record = tree.item(selected_item, 'values')
    image_path = record[8]
    if image_path:
        img = Image.open(image_path)
        img.thumbnail((150, 150))
        img_tk = ImageTk.PhotoImage(img)
        img_label.config(image=img_tk)
        img_label.image = img_tk
    else:
        print("No cover image available")
```

Add an image display label to the GUI:

python

Copy code

```python
img_label = tk.Label(root)
img_label.pack(pady=10)
```

6.3 Handling Edge Cases and Errors

1. Invalid Title for Market Value Fetch:

    Display a message if no results are found:

    python

    Copy code

if market_value is None: print("Market value not found for this title")

2. Invalid Image Upload:

Validate the file type before processing:

python

Copy code

if not file_path.lower().endswith(('.jpg', '.png')): print("Invalid file type. Please upload a JPG or PNG image.") return

3. Missing Fields:

Prevent adding records with empty fields:

python

Copy code

if not title or not publisher: print("Error: All fields are required") return

6.4 Testing the New Features

1. Test the Web-Crawler:

    - Enter a comic title and click Fetch Market Value.
    - Verify that the market value is fetched and displayed correctly.

2. Test Image Upload:

- Upload an image file and ensure it appears in the GUI.
- Add a record with an image and verify that it's saved in the database.

3. Test Integration:

    - Combine the new features with existing CRUD operations.
    - Verify that market values and images are handled correctly during addition, viewing, and deletion of records.

6.5 Enhancing the Features

1. Batch Market Value Fetching:

    Allow users to fetch market values for all records in the database simultaneously.

2. Thumbnail Generation:

    Generate and save thumbnails for uploaded images to improve performance when displaying them in the GUI.

3. Advanced Image Management:

    Allow users to replace or delete cover images for existing records.

4. Web-Crawler Improvements:

    Add support for multiple data sources and merge results to get the most accurate market value.

6.6 What's Next?

With the advanced features implemented, the application is now highly functional. In the next chapter, we'll focus on testing, debugging, and refining the application to ensure a smooth user experience.

Chapter 7: Testing and Debugging

Thorough testing and debugging are critical for ensuring the stability and reliability of your application. In this chapter, we'll cover how to test the comic book database system systematically, debug issues that arise, and refine the application for optimal performance. By the end of this chapter, your application will be polished and ready for deployment.

7.1 The Importance of Testing

Testing ensures that your application functions as intended and provides a good user experience. Key benefits include:

1. Error Detection:

   Identify and fix bugs before users encounter them.

2. Performance Validation:

   Ensure the application responds quickly and handles data efficiently.

3. User Experience:

   Confirm that the application is intuitive and free of critical issues.

7.2 Types of Testing

1. Unit Testing:

   - Focus on individual components (e.g., database operations, GUI elements).
   - Verify that each function behaves as expected.

2. Integration Testing:

   Test how different components work together (e.g., the GUI interacting with the database).

3. System Testing:

   Test the application as a whole, simulating real-world usage.

4. User Testing:

   Have actual users test the application to uncover usability issues.

7.3 Setting Up Unit Tests

Python's built-in unittest module is ideal for testing. Create a tests/ directory in your project and add test scripts for individual components.

Step 1: Testing Database Operations

Write a unit test for the database operations in test_db.py:

python

Copy code

```python
import unittest
import sqlite3

class TestDatabaseOperations(unittest.TestCase):
    def setUp(self):
        # Create a temporary database for testing
        self.conn = sqlite3.connect(":memory:")
        self.cursor = self.conn.cursor()
        self.cursor.execute('''
            CREATE TABLE comic_books (
                id INTEGER PRIMARY KEY AUTOINCREMENT,
                title TEXT,
                publisher TEXT,
                issue TEXT,
                series TEXT,
                face_price REAL,
                quantity INTEGER,
                current_value REAL,
                cover_image TEXT
            )
        ''')
        self.conn.commit()

    def tearDown(self):
        # Close the database connection after each test
        self.conn.close()

    def test_add_comic(self):
        # Add a sample comic
        self.cursor.execute('''
            INSERT INTO comic_books (title, publisher, issue, series, face_price, quantity)
            VALUES (?, ?, ?, ?, ?, ?)
        ''', ("Batman #1", "DC Comics", "1", "Batman", 0.10, 1))
        self.conn.commit()
        # Verify the comic was added
        self.cursor.execute("SELECT * FROM comic_books")
        comics = self.cursor.fetchall()
        self.assertEqual(len(comics), 1)
        self.assertEqual(comics[0][1], "Batman #1")

if __name__ == "__main__":
    unittest.main()
```

Step 2: Run the Tests

Run the test script from the command line:

bash

Copy code

python tests/test_db.py

7.4 Testing the GUI

Testing GUI functionality can be more challenging but is equally important. While manual testing is common for GUI applications, you can automate some aspects.

Manual Testing Checklist:

1. Input Fields:

   - Enter valid and invalid data to test error handling.
   - Verify that fields reset correctly after adding a comic.

2. Buttons:

   - Click each button (e.g., Add, View, Delete) and verify the results.
   - Ensure that disabled buttons become enabled when appropriate.

3. Table Display:

   Verify that the table updates correctly when new data is added, edited, or deleted.

4. Image Upload:

   - Test with valid and invalid file types.
   - Check that uploaded images display properly.

5. Market Value Fetching:

   Test the web-crawler with a variety of comic titles.

7.5 Debugging Common Issues

Here are some common issues you may encounter and how to resolve them:

1. Database Connection Errors:

- Error: sqlite3.OperationalError: database is locked
- Solution: Ensure all database connections are properly closed after operations using conn.close().

2. **GUI Freezing During Web Crawling:**

    - Problem: The application becomes unresponsive while fetching market values.

    - Solution: Use threading to run the web-crawling function in the background:

    ```python
    Copy code


    import threading def fetch_in_background():
    threading.Thread(target=get_current_value).start()
    ```

3. **Incorrect Data Display:**

    - Problem: The table displays outdated data.

    - Solution: Ensure the table is cleared before inserting new data:

    ```python
    Copy code


    tree.delete(*tree.get_children())
    ```

1. **Image Loading Issues:**

    - Problem: Images fail to load or display incorrectly.

- o Solution: Verify the file path and ensure the image exists at the specified location.

7.6 Performance Optimization

1. Optimize Database Queries:

   Use indexes for frequently queried columns (e.g., title, series).

   ```sql
   ```

   Copy code

   CREATE INDEX idx_title ON comic_books (title);

2. Reduce GUI Rendering Time:

   Update only the necessary parts of the GUI instead of re-rendering the entire interface.

3. Efficient Image Handling:

   Resize and compress uploaded images to improve performance:

   ```python
   ```

   Copy code

   img.thumbnail((100, 100), Image.ANTIALIAS)

7.7 User Testing

Once the application is stable, invite users to test it and provide feedback. Focus on:

1. Usability:

    - Are the labels and buttons intuitive?
    - Can users complete tasks without guidance?

2. Aesthetics:

    Does the application look professional and visually appealing?

3. Functionality:

    Does the application meet all user requirements?

7.8 Documenting Bugs and Fixes

Maintain a bug-tracking document to log issues and their resolutions. Include:

- Issue Description: A brief explanation of the problem.
- Steps to Reproduce: How to replicate the issue.
- Resolution: The steps or code changes that resolved the issue.

Example:

IssueSteps to ReproduceResolutionTable not updatingAdd a new comic, then view tableAdd tree.delete(*tree.get_children()) in code.

7.9 Final Testing

Before finalizing the application:

1. Test Across Platforms:

   Run the application on Windows, macOS, and Linux to ensure compatibility.

2. Stress Test:

   Add a large number of records to verify performance and stability.

3. Edge Cases:

   Test unusual inputs, such as very long titles or invalid file paths.

7.10 What's Next?

With a thoroughly tested and debugged application, the next step is to finalize and package the comic book database system for distribution. In the next chapter, we'll focus on packaging the application, adding finishing touches, and preparing it for deployment.

Chapter 8: Finalizing the Application

With the core functionality of the comic book database system implemented and tested, the next step is to finalize the application. This involves polishing the user interface, ensuring compatibility across platforms, and packaging the program for deployment. By the end of this chapter, your application will be ready for distribution and use.

8.1 Polishing the User Interface

A well-designed GUI enhances user experience and makes the application visually appealing. Here are some improvements to consider:

Step 1: Consistent Styling

Apply consistent fonts, colors, and padding throughout the application.

```python
```

Copy code

```python
# Apply consistent styles to all widgets
style = ttk.Style()
style.configure("TLabel", font=("Arial", 12), padding=5)
style.configure("TButton", font=("Arial", 10, "bold"), padding=5)
style.configure("Treeview", font=("Arial", 10))
style.configure("Treeview.Heading", font=("Arial", 12, "bold"))
```

Step 2: Add Icons and Logos

Enhance branding by adding an icon to the application window.

python

Copy code

```
# Set the application icon
root.iconbitmap("icon.ico")
```

Step 3: Create a Welcome Screen

Add a welcome screen or splash screen to introduce the application to users.

python

Copy code

def show_splash_screen(): splash = tk.Toplevel() splash.title("Welcome") splash.geometry("400x300") tk.Label(splash, text="Welcome to the Comic Book Database!", font=("Arial", 16)).pack(pady=50) splash.after(3000, splash.destroy) # Close splash screen after 3 seconds show_splash_screen()

8.2 Ensuring Compatibility

1. Cross-Platform Testing:

    o Test the application on Windows, macOS, and Linux to ensure compatibility.
    o Verify that paths, fonts, and other OS-specific features work seamlessly.

2. Resolution and Scaling:

    o Ensure the application scales properly on different screen resolutions.
    o Use geometry to define responsive window sizes.

8.3 Enhancing User Experience

Step 1: Add Help and Documentation

Include a "Help" menu or button in the GUI.

python

Copy code

def show_help(): help_window = tk.Toplevel() help_window.title("Help") help_window.geometry("500x400") tk.Label(help_window, text="How to Use the Comic Book Database", font=("Arial", 14)).pack(pady=10) tk.Text(help_window, wrap="word", height=20).pack(fill="both", expand=True)

Add the help menu to the main window:

python

Copy code

menu_bar = tk.Menu(root) help_menu = tk.Menu(menu_bar, tearoff=0) help_menu.add_command(label="How to Use", command=show_help) menu_bar.add_cascade(label="Help", menu=help_menu) root.config(menu=menu_bar)

Step 2: Provide Feedback for User Actions

Add confirmation messages for actions like adding or deleting a record:

```
python
```

Copy code

from tkinter import messagebox def add_comic(): # Add record to the database... messagebox.showinfo("Success", "Comic added successfully!")

8.4 Packaging the Application

To share your application, you'll package it as an executable file that runs without requiring Python to be installed on the user's system.

Step 1: Install PyInstaller

PyInstaller converts Python scripts into standalone executables:

bash

Copy code

pip install pyinstaller

Step 2: Create the Executable

Run the following command in the terminal:

bash

Copy code

pyinstaller --onefile --windowed main.py

- --onefile: Bundles everything into a single executable file.
- --windowed: Suppresses the console window (for GUI apps).

The executable will be located in the dist/ folder.

8.5 Adding Finishing Touches

1. Include Sample Data:

   Provide pre-loaded sample data for users to explore.

2. Bundle Dependencies:

   Ensure all required libraries and resources (e.g., images, icons) are included in the package.

3. Add a README File:

   Include a README.md file with instructions for installing and using the application.

8.6 Deployment Options

1. Local Distribution:

Share the executable via email, USB drive, or file-sharing platforms.

2. Online Hosting:

   Host the application on platforms like GitHub or Google Drive for easy download.

3. App Stores:

   Package the application for distribution on app stores like the Microsoft Store or Mac App Store.

8.7 Testing the Final Package

1. Run the Executable:

   Test the packaged application on different systems to ensure it works correctly.

2. Check for Missing Files:

   Verify that all required files (e.g., database, images) are included.

3. Test User Scenarios:

   Simulate common user actions to confirm the application behaves as expected.

8.8 Enhancing for Future Versions

1. Add User Authentication:

Implement login functionality for managing user accounts.

2. Cloud Integration:

   Sync the database with cloud storage for remote access.

3. Advanced Search and Filtering:

   Allow users to filter comics by multiple criteria (e.g., publisher and series).

4. Mobile-Friendly Version:

   Develop a mobile app version of the database.

8.9 What's Next?

Congratulations! Your comic book database system is complete and ready for use. In the next chapter, we'll reflect on the development process, summarize what you've learned, and explore ideas for expanding your skills further.

Chapter 9: Conclusion and Next Steps

With the comic book database application complete, it's time to reflect on what we've accomplished, summarize the key skills and concepts you've learned, and explore how you can expand and enhance your project. This chapter will guide you on how to take the skills you've developed to the next level and explore further opportunities in software development.

9.1 Summary of the Project

The comic book database application combines various programming concepts, tools, and techniques into a cohesive and functional system. Here's an overview of what we built:

1. Database Management:

    - Designed a relational database schema using SQLite.
    - Implemented CRUD (Create, Read, Update, Delete) operations.

2. Graphical User Interface (GUI):

    - Built a user-friendly interface using Tkinter.
    - Integrated input fields, buttons, and a table view for seamless interaction.

3. Web-Crawling Feature:

    Developed a web crawler to fetch real-time market values of comic books using requests and BeautifulSoup.

4. Image Handling:

    Enabled users to upload, store, and display comic book cover images with the Pillow library.

5. Testing and Debugging:

   Applied unit and integration testing to ensure application stability and reliability.

6. Packaging and Deployment:

   Packaged the application into a standalone executable for easy distribution.

9.2 Key Skills and Concepts Learned

1. Python Programming:

   - Mastered functions, classes, file handling, and error handling.
   - Leveraged Python's extensive library ecosystem for database management, GUI creation, and web scraping.

2. Database Design:

   - Learned how to design and implement a database schema.
   - Gained experience in executing SQL commands and managing data effectively.

3. GUI Development:

   - Built a responsive and intuitive interface using Tkinter.
   - Managed user interactions with widgets like Entry, Button, and Treeview.

4. Web Scraping:

Extracted and parsed data from web pages using requests and BeautifulSoup.

5. Image Processing:

   Implemented image upload and display functionality with the Pillow library.

6. Software Testing:

   - Wrote unit tests to validate individual components.
   - Debugged and resolved common application issues.

1. Software Packaging:

   Used PyInstaller to create a standalone executable for distribution.

9.3 Challenges and Solutions

1. Database Locking Errors:

   Solution: Ensured all database connections were closed properly using conn.close().

2. Unresponsive GUI During Web Crawling:

   Solution: Used threading to run the web-crawling function in the background.

3. Invalid User Inputs:

   Solution: Added input validation and error messages to guide users.

4. Image Display Issues:

   Solution: Resized and compressed images using Pillow to improve performance.

9.4 Ideas for Future Enhancements

While the current application is functional, there's always room for improvement. Here are some ideas to expand its features and functionality:

1. User Authentication:

   Add login functionality to manage multiple user accounts and restrict access to specific features.

2. Cloud Integration:

   Sync the database with a cloud service (e.g., Firebase, AWS RDS) to enable remote access.

3. Advanced Search Filters:

   Allow users to filter records by multiple criteria (e.g., price range, publisher, series).

4. Reporting and Analytics:

   Add features to generate reports, such as the total value of a comic collection or trends in market values.

5. Export and Import:

Enable users to export data to CSV or Excel files and import data from external sources.

6. Mobile and Web Versions:

   Develop a mobile app or web-based version of the database for accessibility across devices.

1. Dark Mode:

   Add a toggle for dark mode to enhance user experience.

9.5 Exploring Further Opportunities

1. Expand Your Knowledge of Python:

   Learn advanced Python concepts like multithreading, decorators, and asynchronous programming.

2. Master Other GUI Frameworks:

   Explore other GUI frameworks like PyQt, Kivy, or wxPython to create more sophisticated interfaces.

3. Learn Full-Stack Development:

   Combine your Python skills with web technologies (e.g., HTML, CSS, JavaScript) to create web-based applications.

4. Explore Data Science and Machine Learning:

   Use Python libraries like Pandas, NumPy, and Scikit-learn to analyze comic book market trends.

5. Contribute to Open Source:

   Share your project on GitHub and collaborate with other developers to enhance it further.

6. Build a Portfolio:

   Use this project as a portfolio piece to showcase your skills to potential employers or clients.

9.6 Sharing Your Application

1. Upload to GitHub:

   Share your code repository on GitHub for others to view, download, and contribute.

2. Distribute the Executable:

   Share the packaged application via platforms like Dropbox, Google Drive, or your personal website.

3. Seek Feedback:

   Share your application with friends, family, or online communities (e.g., Reddit, Python forums) to gather feedback and improve.

9.7 Final Thoughts

Completing this project demonstrates your ability to design and develop a comprehensive software application from start to finish. By integrating concepts like database management, GUI development, and web scraping, you've created a practical tool that solves a real-world problem.

9.8 What's Next?

Your journey doesn't have to end here. Consider applying what you've learned to new projects, such as:

- A personal library management system.
- A recipe database with nutritional analysis.
- A fitness tracker with data visualization.

The skills you've developed through this project will serve as a solid foundation for tackling even more ambitious software development challenges.

www.ingramcontent.com/pod-product-compliance
Lightning Source LLC
Chambersburg PA
CBHW071654240526
45469CB00023B/2372